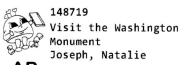

D1567238

WATERS ELEMENTARY SCHOOL
MEDIA CENTER

Visit the
WASHINGTON
MONUMENT

By Natalie Joseph

Gareth Stevens
Publishing

Please visit our website, www.garethstevens.com. For a free color catalog of all our high-quality books, call toll free 1-800-542-2595 or fax 1-877-542-2596.

Library of Congress Cataloging-in-Publication Data

Joseph, Natalie.
Visit the Washington Monument / Natalie Joseph.
    p. cm. — (Landmarks of liberty)
Includes index.
ISBN 978-1-4339-6406-0 (pbk.)
ISBN 978-1-4339-6407-7 (6 pack)
ISBN 978-1-4339-6404-6 (library binding)
1. Washington Monument (Washington, D.C.)—Juvenile literature. 2. Washington, George, 1732-1799—Monuments—Washington (D.C.)—Juvenile literature. 3. Washington (D.C.)—Buildings, structures, etc.—Juvenile literature. I. Title.
F203.4.W3J75 2012
975.3—dc23

2011036112

First Edition

Published in 2012 by
Gareth Stevens Publishing
111 East 14th Street, Suite 349
New York, NY 10003

Designer: Andrea Davison-Bartolotta
Editor: Therese Shea

Photo credits: Cover (except main image), back cover (all), (pp. 2-3, 21, 22-23, 24 flag background), (pp. 4-21 corkboard background), pp. 4, 5 (both), 19 Shutterstock.com; cover (main image), p. 1 iStockphoto.com; p. 7 SuperStock/Getty Images; p. 9 Universal Hulton Archive/Getty Images; p. 11 MPI/Getty Images; p. 13 Hulton Archive/Getty Images; p. 15 Tim Sloan/AFP/Getty Images; p. 17 (main image) Buenlarge/Getty Images; p. 17 (inset) Comstock Images/Thinkstock; p. 20 Andy Dunaway/USAF via Getty Images.

Printed in the United States of America

CPSIA compliance information: Batch #CW12GS: For further information contact Gareth Stevens, New York, New York at 1-800-542-2595.

Contents

Words in the glossary appear in **bold** type the first time they are used in the text.

Pick a President!

If someone asked you to think of a past US president, who would come to mind? Most people would say George Washington. Founding father, military leader, and farmer, Washington was a greatly respected figure in his own time. Few could imagine another man as our nation's first president.

Today, the pencil-shaped monument that bears Washington's name is one of the most noticeable and beloved in Washington, DC. It's both tall and striking, much like the man himself.

Many paintings show Washington as a military hero on horseback. The Washington Monument is shown at right.

Early Years

George Washington was born February 22, 1732. Growing up in the Virginia colony, he loved exploring the countryside. At first, Washington wanted to be a sailor. He decided later to be a **surveyor**. He traveled the wilderness of Virginia for several years.

When Washington was 20 years old, he joined the Virginia **militia**. He fought for the British during the French and Indian War (1754–1763). Though he was often on the losing side of the battle, his soldiers praised his bravery.

Tell Me More!

After a battle to control Fort Duquesne in Pennsylvania, George Washington said, "I luckily escaped without a wound, though I had four bullets through my coat and two horses shot under me."

Washington is shown here surveying land in Virginia's Shenandoah Valley. Some of his surveying tools are still displayed at his home in Mount Vernon.

The Coming Conflict

By the late 1760s, England was passing laws that stripped American colonists of certain rights. Washington believed the colonists might have to fight for their freedom.

Washington attended the First **Continental Congress** in 1774 as a **representative** of Virginia. Other representatives valued his common sense and military knowledge. The colonies' fight for freedom began in 1775. The Second Continental Congress chose Washington as commander in chief of the colonial army by a **unanimous** vote.

Tell Me More!

When Washington was chosen to lead the colonial army, he refused a salary for his service.

Washington and many others at the Second Continental Congress didn't want war. They felt they had no other choice.

Winning the War

Washington's colonial army—called the Continental army—was mostly made up of poorly trained militiamen. It was much smaller than the British army. The Americans often ran out of supplies, too. Many soldiers ran away. Still, Washington believed that the Americans could win, especially with France's help.

In September 1781, Washington surrounded 8,000 British troops stationed in Yorktown, Virginia. England soon decided to allow the colonies—the United States—their freedom. Washington returned to his family and farm, called Mount Vernon.

Tell Me More!

After the American **Revolution**, some suggested that Washington be made king of the new country. He refused.

In this image, British general Lord Cornwallis surrenders to Washington at Yorktown. In real life, Cornwallis refused to meet with Washington, making his second in command present the "sword of surrender."

11

President Washington

In 1787, Washington attended the **Constitutional Convention** as a Virginia representative. He was elected president of the convention. The new US Constitution approved by the representatives called for three branches of government, including a president.

In 1789, the first presidential election was held. George Washington received the largest number of votes possible. As he traveled to New York City, the US capital at that time, Americans lined the road cheering. Washington tried to be a fair president. He didn't want the president to have too much power.

Tell Me More!

Washington didn't want to serve a second term as president. However, Thomas Jefferson told him that he was the only man who could keep the young country together.

Washington was sworn in as president of the United States on April 30, 1789.

A New Capital

In 1790, Washington was given the power to choose a new site for the nation's capital. He chose an area near his home in Virginia. He appointed Pierre L'Enfant to **design** the capital city. L'Enfant made sure there was a special place in his plans for a monument honoring Washington.

After his presidency, Washington went back to his farm. He enjoyed being with his family and farming again. He died on December 14, 1799, after a short illness. People all over the world were saddened.

Tell Me More!

The new capital city was given the name Washington in 1791. The area surrounding it was named the **District** of Columbia after Christopher Columbus.

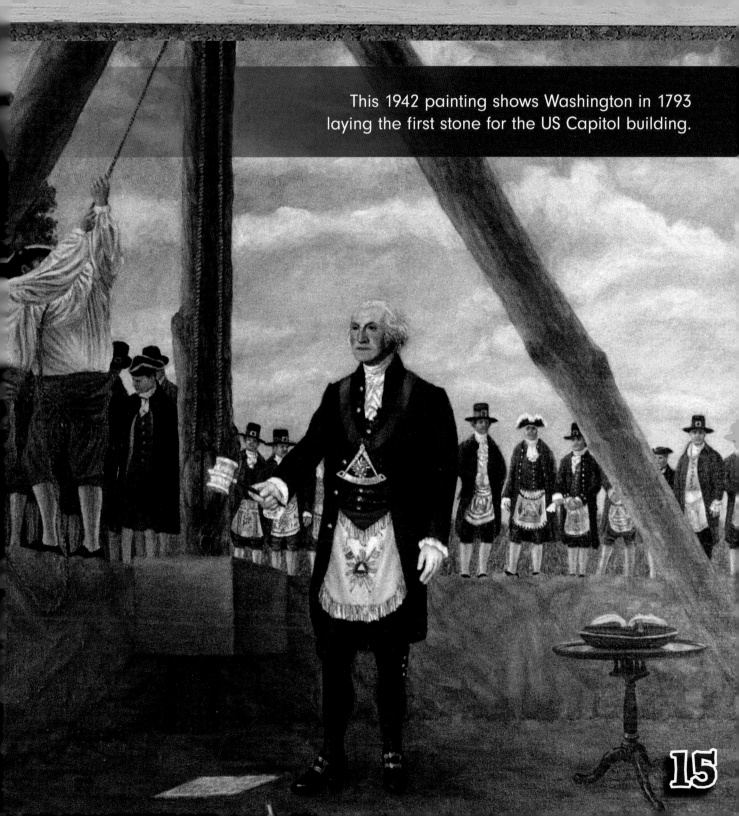

This 1942 painting shows Washington in 1793 laying the first stone for the US Capitol building.

Stone by Stone

The plan for Washington's monument was not officially approved until 1836. The Washington National Monument Society chose the design of Robert Mills. He wanted the monument to be an **obelisk**—much like the obelisks of ancient Egypt. The first stone was laid July 4, 1848.

People donated, or gave, stones to build the obelisk, but work was slow. Donations nearly stopped in 1855 when a group of people stole a valuable stone sent from Rome, Italy. Work stopped again between 1861 and 1865, the years of the American Civil War.

Tell Me More!

After the first stone of the Washington Monument was laid, they had to move the monument north because the ground was too soft at the original location.

The photo on the right shows the Washington Monument in 1864, when work had been stopped during the Civil War.

Eygptian obelisks

17

Standing Tall

The Washington Monument was completed in 1884. It stands 555 feet 5 1/18 inches (169.29 m) tall. At the base, each side measures 55 feet 1 1/2 inches (16.8 m) long. The walls are covered with white marble from Maryland.

The Washington Monument is hollow. On the inside walls are 193 stones with **carvings** on them. These were donations, too.

The tip of the monument has a cap made of aluminum. When the monument was built, aluminum was very valuable.

The monument has an elevator inside that takes people to the top.

On a clear day, visitors can see more than 30 miles (48 km) away from the top of the monument.

SOUTH

A U.S. Holocaust Memorial Museum
B Bureau of Engraving & Printing
C Washington Channel
D East Potomac Park
E Potomac River
F Reagan Washington National Airport
G Jefferson Memorial
H Tidal Basin

1 9 9 9

1 9 1 4

Visiting the Washington Monument

In 2011, an East Coast earthquake cracked the top of the monument. Officials closed the monument for a time due to safety concerns. The Washington Monument is usually open every day of the year except July 4 and December 25.

The monument is part of the National Mall, which is a rectangular strip of land where many other monuments and buildings have been built. The Washington Monument is located near the center, between the Lincoln Memorial and the US Capitol.

Today, the Washington Monument is cared for by the National Park Service.

Timeline of the Washington Monument

1732	George Washington is born February 22.
1752	Washington joins the Virginia militia.
1775	Washington is named commander in chief of the Continental army.
1789	Washington is elected president of the United States.
1799	Washington dies December 14.
1836	The design for the Washington Monument is approved.
1848	The first stone is laid for the Washington Monument.
1884	The Washington Monument is completed.

Glossary

carving: an object formed by cutting and shaping a material such as stone

Constitutional Convention: a meeting that took place in 1787 to address problems in the original US constitution

Continental Congress: a meeting of colonial representatives before, during, and after the American Revolution

design: to plan the pattern or shape of something. Also, the pattern or shape of it.

district: an area with a special feature or government

militia: an army made up of citizens with military training who serve only when they are needed

obelisk: a column of stone with a square base, sides that slope in, and a pyramid on top

representative: a member of a lawmaking body who acts for voters

revolution: the overthrow of a government

surveyor: one whose job is to measure land areas

unanimous: with all members in agreement

For More Information

Books

Harris, Nancy. *Washington Monument*. Chicago, IL: Heinemann-Raintree, 2008.

Landau, Elaine. *The Washington Monument*. New York, NY: Children's Press, 2004.

Schaffer, Julia. *The Washington Monument*. New York, NY: Chelsea Clubhouse, 2010.

Websites

George Washington
www.whitehouse.gov/about/presidents/georgewashington
Read more about the life of George Washington.

Washington Monument
www.nps.gov/wamo/
Plan your trip to visit the Washington Monument

Index